Praise for

"Jared and Megan Kennedy have written a treasure of a book — a 40-page wonder that will instruct and guide your church in every aspect of a child dedication service."

> **Robert L. Plummer,** Ph.D., Professor of New Testament Interpretation, The Southern Baptist Theological Seminary

"Whenever I teach about training parents to disciple their children, I emphasize the opportunity that child dedication services can provide—and someone inevitably asks me, 'Can you recommend a simple guide for doing that in our church?' Now, I can say, 'Yes, there is one.' Megan and Jared Kennedy have provided a simple, theologically-grounded guide for churches to follow as they seek to train parents to disciple their children."

> **Timothy Paul Jones,** Ph.D., Professor of Family Ministry, The Southern Baptist Theological Seminary; author of *Family Ministry Field Guide* and *The God Who Goes Before You*

"Jared does more than present a path for leading child dedications. He suggests a commitment for rooting parenthood in the gospel and sound theology. This resource will be so beneficial to churches as they partner with parents for the sake of the gospel."

> **Jenny Funderburke Smith,** Minister to Children, West Bradenton Baptist Church and blogger, Gospelatcenter.com

"Many churches, seeking to honor parent and celebrate the gift of new life, hold Child Dedication services that are little more than pageantry. In *Before the Church, Before the Lord*, Jared and Megan Kennedy have given a thoroughly insightful, biblical, theological, and practical resource to help churches shape these celebrations into meaningful times of worship. I highly recommend it!"

John Murchison, Director of Austin Stone Resources, The Austin Stone Community Church

"*Before the Church, Before the Lord* is a spiritually rich and refreshingly practical resource for any parents considering child dedication and any church that wants to grow this important covenantal opportunity. Jared and Megan Kennedy's high view of God, children and the body of Christ shine through as they discuss biblical parental stewardship. Now please excuse me while I go recommend this fantastic tool to my church!"

Joshua Cooley, Children's Minister and author of *The Biggest Win, Heroes of the Bible Devotional* and *The One Year Devotions with Jesus*

"While parents are called to raise their children in the discipline and instruction of the Lord, the church also has a God-given role in walking alongside them as a covenant community. *Before the Lord, Before the Church* is a valuable resource for churches seeking to do just that. The philosophy and practices outlined in this book provide a useful roadmap that will equip churches to help parents point their children to God's redeeming love."

Scott James, elder at The Church at Brook Hills, author of *The Littlest Watchman: Watching and Waiting for the Very First Christmas, The Expected One: Anticipating All of Jesus in the Advent,* and *Mission Accomplished: A Two-Week Family Easter Devotional*

Praise for the "How-To" Series

"The Sojourn Network 'How-To' books are a great combination of biblical theology and practical advice, driven by a commitment to the gospel and the local congregation. Written by the local church for the local church — just the job!"

> **Tim Chester**, pastor of Grace Church Boroughbridge,
> faculty member of Crosslands Training, and author
> of over 40 books

"This series brings pastoral wisdom for everyday life in the church of Jesus Christ. Think of these short, practical books as the equivalent of a healthy breakfast, a sandwich and apple for lunch, and a family enjoying dinner together. The foundational theology is nutritious, and the practical applications will keep the body strong."

> **Dr. David Powlison**, Executive Director of CCEF;
> senior editor, Journal of Biblical Counseling; author
> of *Good and Angry: Redeeming Anger* and *Making All
> Things New: Restoring Joy to the Sexually Broken*

"Most leaders don't need another abstract book on leadership; we need help with the 'how-to's.' And my friends in the Sojourn Network excel in this area. I've been well served by their practical ministry wisdom, and I know you will be too."

> **Bob Thune**, Founding Pastor, Coram Deo Church,
> Omaha, NE, author of *Gospel Eldership* and co-
> author of *The Gospel-Centered Life*

"I cannot express strong enough what a valuable resource this is for church planters, church planting teams and young churches. The topics that are addressed in these books are so needed in young churches. I have been in ministry and missions for over 30 years and I learned a lot from reading. Very engaging and very practical!"

Larry McCrary, Co-Founder and Director of The Upstream Collective

"There are many aspects of pastoral ministry that aren't (and simply can't) be taught in seminary. Even further, many pastors simply don't have the benefit of a brotherhood of pastors that they can lean on to help them navigate topics such as building a healthy plurality of elders or working with artists in the church. I'm thankful for the men and women who labored to produce this series, which is both theologically-driven and practically-minded. The Sojourn Network "How-To" series is a great resource for pastors and church planters alike."

Jamaal Williams, Lead Pastor of Sojourn Midtown, Louisville, KY

BEFORE -THE- Lord, BEFORE -THE- Church

Jared Kennedy with Megan Kennedy

Series Editor: Dave Harvey

Before the Lord, Before the Church
"How-To" Plan a Child Dedication Service

© 2018 Jared Kennedy with Megan Kennedy
All rights reserved.

A publication of Sojourn Network Press in Louisville, KY. For more books by Sojourn Network, visit us at sojournnetwork.com/store.

Cover design: Josh Noom & Benjamin Vrbicek
Interior design: Benjamin Vrbicek

Trade paperback ISBN: 978-1732055254

The Sojourn Network book series is dedicated to the pastors, elders, and deacons of Sojourn Network churches. Because you are faithful, the church will be served and sent as we plant, grow, and multiply healthy churches that last.

CONTENTS

"Our Kids Belong to God"
"We Will Commit to Love"
"We Need the Church"

1. Why Do You Perform Child Dedications Rather than
   Infant Baptisms?
2. Is this Even biblical?
3. Why Do We Need a Service to Be Dedicated?
4. Isn't this just a Sentimental Exercise?

Annually; 12 Weeks Before; 6–8 Weeks Before; 2 Weeks
    Before; Sunday Before (Child Dedication Class); 1–
    Week Prior; and On Dedication Sunday
Four Mistakes of Child Dedication
Four Keys of Child Dedication

SERIES PREFACE

Why should the Sojourn Network publish a "How-To" series?

It's an excellent question, since it leads to a more personal and pertinent question for you: *Why should you bother to read any of these books?*

Sojourn Network, the ministry I am honored to lead, exists to plant, grow, and multiply healthy networks, churches, and pastors. Therefore, it seems only natural to convert some of our leader's best thinking and practices into written material focusing on the "How-To" aspects of local church ministry and multiplication.

We love church planters and church planting. But we've come to believe it's not enough to do assessments and fund church plants. We must also help, equip, and learn from one another in order to be good shepherds and leaders. We must stir up one another to the good work of leading churches towards their most fruitful future.

That's why some books will lend themselves to soul calibration for ministry longevity, while others will examine the riggings of specific ministries or specialized mission. This is essential work to building ministries *that last.* But God has also placed it on our hearts to share our mistakes and most fruitful practices so that others might improve upon what we have done. This way, everyone wins.

If our prayer is answered, this series will bring thoughtful, pastoral, charitable, gospel-saturated, church-grounded, renewal-based "practice" to the rhythms of local church life and network collaboration.

May these "How-To" guides truly serve you. May they arm you with new ideas for greater leadership effectiveness. Finally, may they inspire you to love Jesus more and serve his people with grace-inspired gladness, in a ministry that passes the test of time.

Dave Harvey
President, Sojourn Network

INTRODUCTORY LETTER

He established a testimony in Jacob
and appointed a law in Israel,
which he commanded our fathers
to teach to their children,
that the next generation might know them,
the children yet unborn,
and arise and tell them to their children,
so that they should set their hope in God
and not forget the works of God,
but keep his commandments." (Psalm 78:5–7)

Dear Church Leader,

In Psalm 78:7, we see God's desire for every generation. God wants kids to put their hope in him. He wants them to know and trust in him. Specifically, God wants them to not forget what he's done to rescue and save us. Instead, he wants the next generation to remember his words and obey them.

Since you're reading this book, this is likely your desire as well. But how will that desire be fulfilled? Psalm 78 is not a pipe dream. It's a God-given responsibility for parents and the church.

The primary context for our kids learning about God is not in children's ministry on Sundays. Instead, our homes, our cars as we drive along the road, by our child's bedside, and at the breakfast table — will be our lecture halls and laboratories. These are the places our children will hear and see the gospel. Discipleship happens in planned moments when we pull out a Bible storybook and in unplanned moments when our child sins or is heartbroken, and we give correction and comfort.

This psalm charges parents with this responsibility, but it also tells us that God gave his people a community. Training kids doesn't end with parents; it includes the whole church. We need each other. We need one another's encouragement, one another's accountability, and one another's eyes to see what we can't see. Without understanding the role of the church, child dedications make no sense.

> **Training kids doesn't end with parents; it includes the whole church.**

Therefore, we conduct child dedication services for three reasons:

- First, God wants our kids, and ultimately their hearts and lives, to belong to him. So, in dedication we confess together, "God, all we have — even our children — belongs to you. All we have is yours."

- Second, we don't just dedicate our children. We dedicate ourselves. We do this because we recognize our God-given responsibility as parents.
- Third, we dedicate to ask for help in the form of a commitment from our church, the believing community.

The notes in this book unpack each of these three reasons with more detail. Our prayer is that the Holy Spirit uses the teaching you encounter here to inspire and encourage you as you prepare and plan a child dedication service for your church community.

With joy in Christ,
Jared Kennedy
Children's & Family Ministry Strategist for Sojourn Network

PHILOSOPHY (PART 1)

TWO TRIPS TO THE GROCERY STORE: A THEOLOGY OF CHILD DEDICATION

Imagine heading over to your local grocery store. You pick up milk, bread, and eggs. You've got your kids in tow so you're relieved when you can navigate the aisles without incident. You head to the checkout counter. The cashier rings up your items and delivers the total. You swipe your card, she thanks you for shopping and hands you a receipt. As you walk out toward the parking lot, you look it over. A pretty normal trip to the grocer.

In the Bible, there are two basic kinds of relationship — contract relationships and covenant relationships.[1] A for-profit business — like a grocery store or coffee shop — typifies the *contract* relationship. A barista at your local coffee shop provides you with an espresso, and you leave a few dollars for your caffeine indulgence. In a contract negotiation,

---

[1] Peter J. Gentry and Stephen J. Wellum, *Kingdom through Covenant: A Biblical-Theological Understanding of the Covenants* (Wheaton: Crossway, 2012), 140–141.

an arrival at a mutually satisfactory agreement is essential. Like buying a car, it's important to settle on a price before you drive it off the lot.

Contracts have obligations and conditions that *require* performance. The terms must be fulfilled. If I go into business with you and I break one of the terms of our contract, our business relationship is over. And even when all of the terms are kept, some contracts — like the fading ink on a receipt — only last for a specified period of time. Because the parties in a contract are consumers, I may choose to break my contract intentionally if it no longer benefits me. Tim Keller describes it this way:

> In a consumer relationship, it could be said that the individual's needs are more important than the relationship.[2]

If the grocery store down the street offers better quality produce or double coupons, I may alter my buying habits.

Now imagine a different trip to the store. This time, everyone there greets you by name when you arrive. When you head to the checkout, the manager begins to recount the history of your relationship with the store: "Donna first visited this location in 2005. She picked up puréed squash, peas, and bananas for her six-month-old. We remember it like yesterday." At this point, you're thinking, "I know that they keep my purchase history on my Bonus Card, but this is a little creepy." Suddenly you see the manager is no longer

---

[2] Timothy Keller, *The Meaning of Marriage: Facing the Complexities of Commitment with the Wisdom of God* (New York: Dutton, 2011), 81.

reminiscing. He has his right hand raised, and he's swearing an oath. We solemnly swear to provide you with non-GMO snack food choices and the most delectable selection of meats. Furthermore, today's shopping trip is our *gift* to you. We're family. Take whatever you like."

To put it mildly, this is not a normal day at your grocery store.

This second trip is more like a *covenantal* relationship, which arises out of a personal history and the intention for deeper intimacy. In a covenant, negotiation has no place. The stronger party, that is, the party who is greater in grace, makes a proposal and gives his friendship and help as a gift. Covenant relationships aren't even maintained by performance. If I break promises that I've made to my wife Megan — like failing to love and cherish her well when she is sick — that doesn't mean that our marriage is over. It means I better improve. Our relationship is rooted in something deeper — a covenant — and it is maintained by loyalty and unconditional love.

Sociologists report that the marketplace has become so dominant in our society that the consumer model increasingly characterizes most relationships. Slipping into this mindset with our kids is easy. We parent with our hearts set on "getting the right return on our investment." When our children are cute and we're posting fun pictures of family night on Instagram, we feel good. But, when the kids are screaming and pitching a fit on aisle 7, we may feel like cutting our losses.

SIDEBAR A: CONTRACT VS. COVENANT	
Contract	**Covenant**
"I want a product or service."	"I want a relationship."
Thing-oriented	Person-oriented
Requires Performance	Requires Loyalty and Love

In those moments, we must remember kids aren't commodities, burdens, or opportunities to seize. Children are gifts from God (Psalm 127:3), not the products of our success. They weren't given to us to improve our portfolio and enhance our personal success. We have a daily responsibility to press in with unconditional covenant loyalty and love. We can do this, because we have a heavenly Father who loves us, his children, in the same way. He keeps covenant with us even when we close our ears to his instruction and pitch fits about what he commands and forbids. He loved us with sacrificial, covenant love even when we were still sinners (Romans 5:8).

> **Children are gifts from God, not the products of our success.**

So, how do we build our churches towards parenting with a covenant mentality?

- First, we need to invite parents to confess, "Our kids don't belong to us. They belong to God."
- Second, we call them to make a biblical commitment to love their kids even when times get tough.

- Finally, we need to help parents see and confess their need for the church because we can't parent alone.

Let's take each of these three invitations in turn.

"Our Kids Belong to God"

Parents are responsible to provide and care for their children. We are on the front line as their primary disciplers. But, in these responsibilities, parents are *stewards*. God calls parents to faithfulness with their kids, not possession of them. Our kids ultimately belong to a promise-keeping God who will be infinitely more faithful than us. As Psalm 127 says, our children are a heritage from their Lord; they are an unmerited reward from him.

> **Our kids ultimately belong to a promise-keeping God who will be infinitely more faithful than us.**

SIDEBAR B: SENTIMENTAL VISION VS. STEWARDSHIP VISION	
Sentimental Vision	Stewardship Vision
"This kid is mine."	"My kid belongs to God."
"Always my little prince or princess."	"I will commit to love."
"My family and our values are enough."	"I need the church."

The older your kids get, the more it becomes clear that we can't control their course. It rests in *their* hearts, not *our* hands. Our kids' future, their health, their skill, their will and desires for life, who they will choose as a spouse, and even how long they will live — all of this belongs to God.

One enemy of stewardship is a subtle, sneaky, sentimentalism. An entitled dad with a sentimental vision says, "This kid is *mine*. He's going to be just like me. He's going to be into the music I like. He's going to love Alabama football just like I do." But when that dad's expectations aren't met and his kids don't turn out the way he hoped, he's angry. And he no longer knows how to engage his child. The entitled mom expects the times she shares together with her children will always be Hallmark precious. When her hopes are dashed, she says, "I deserve better than this. Don't you know how I suffered to bring you into the world." When her teenager rebels, she can turn bitter and feel as if God is letting her down. He isn't upholding his part of the bargain.

A stewardship vision of parenting — one that says my kids belong to God — is scary, because God doesn't always meet our expectations. God does not operate the world according to our vision of satisfaction or success, nor should he. Paul Miller writes about how we're tempted to shy away when confronted with suffering:

> Many years ago when our daughter Kim was born with multiple disabilities, some of my wife's friends found her grief overwhelming and pulled back. It was too hard to bear with someone who problems didn't go away

quickly. We've not been taught that to love someone means we enter their suffering. We don't realize that the normal Christian life is to "share [Jesus's] sufferings, becoming like him in his death" (Philippians 3:10). So when faced with a problem that wouldn't go away (Kim) and a raw broken heart (Jill), some pulled away.[3]

God's vision for our lives, even when it takes a cruciform shape, is more perfect than ours. Ultimately, accepting this truth is freeing, and it will lead us to gratitude.

A covenant way of thinking frees us from the pressure to get everything right with our parenting. In a fallen world, some kids *will* be sick and some kids *will* fall away from the faith. We can never accomplish all of our good goals for their health, education, manners, and athletics. A stewardship vision frees us to be thankful and enjoy God's good gifts when do they come because our children (and all good things they bring into our lives) are gifts from God. As Paul says in 1 Corinthians 4:7, "What do you have that you did not receive?"

Child dedication helps us pause and begin to cultivate an attitude of grateful stewardship. It's a way of publicly celebrating the good gift of children before our people. It's a way of practicing gratitude for our kids rather than complaining about them. It's also a public confession that any good (or any pain!) we receive at our kids' hands comes from the God who gave them to us.

---

[3] Paul Miller, *A Loving Life: In a World of Broken Relationships* (Wheaton: Crossway, 2014), 50.

"We Will Commit to Love"

Let's face it. Babies are beautiful. During our child dedication services, our congregations will ooh and ah over the baby photos on the big screen. But consider James K. A. Smith's perspective given to the parents of a young child named Liam:

> While I don't mean to rain on the parade of your joy, I do feel compelled to share the bad news, too: Liam might break your heart. Actually, Liam *is* going to break your heart. Somehow. Somewhere. Maybe more than once. To become a parent is to promise that you'll love prodigals. Indeed, some days parenting is exactly how God is going to teach you to love your enemies . . . It will require absorbing all of Liam's misplaced animosity, all his confused attempts to figure out who (and whose) he is. At those moments, Jesus's call to lay down your life and take up the cross with have a mundane tangibility you could have never imagined.[4]

Smith's words are a helpful warning against the kind of sentimentalism which envisions parenting as a cuddly advert for Baby Gap and then gives up when broken and sinful kids don't live up to that dream. We must spur parents toward faithful, committed love even in the midst of disappointment, pain, and suffering. Parents need to see that committed love conquers all — even when it feels like your toddler is conquering you.

---

[4] James K. A. Smith, "Letter to a Young Parent," Comment Magazine, March 1, 2011, https://www.cardus.ca/comment/article/2804/letter-to-a-young-parent/.

In the Hebrew of the Old Testament, there is a word pair consistently used to express loyalty to sworn oaths and covenant promises — *hesed* and *emet*. Sometimes English versions translate those terms "love and faithfulness" (Exodus 34:6; Proverbs 3:3). The Greek equivalents are translated "grace and truth" (John 1:14, 17). I've been using the term "committed" or "loyal love."[5]

Twice each year at Sojourn Community Church, we call parents to committed, loyal love through the solemn covenant ceremony of child dedication. And you know what's interesting? Of all of the things we do in children's ministry, this is the one event that I get the most questions about from church planters: "Why does your church do child dedications? I don't see that in the Bible."

> **Parents need to see that committed love conquers all — even when it feels like your toddler is conquering you.**

I have to be honest with you. I don't have any verses either. I can't point to a passage which says, "Thou shalt have child dedication services." But I do know parents are tempted to think about their relationship with their kids as if it was a contract. And I also know nothing challenges consumer thinking quite as much as making difficult covenant promises. This is true for marriage, and it's true for parenting too. The child dedication covenant confirms the reality: parenting is a higher, self-sacrificial commitment. The solemn public vow helps us teach parents to practice regular patterns of sacrificial love from the very beginning of their parenting journey.

---

5 Gentry and Wellum, *Kingdom through Covenant*, 141–145.

When God rescued Israel from Egypt, he gave them a whole catalog of laws, ceremonies, and sacrifices to help them remember his great rescue, confirm his covenant relationship, and guide their journey to the Promised Land. He gave them patterns and practices. These traditions were important because God wanted Israel's faith to be passed down to their children (Psalm 78).

SIDEBAR C: SAMPLE <u>PARENT</u> VOWS FOR CHILD DEDICATION

Parents, will you entrust your children to God — to his providential plan and care?

Will you commit, with the help of this church community, to instruct your children by word and example, in the truth God's Word?

Will you commit to pray for them and teach them to pray?
If so, say, "<u>With God's help, we will.</u>"

God gives us patterns for life as New Testament Christians as well. Parents who participate in our child dedication services commit to instruct, discipline, teach, and pray for their kids. Committing to all this may sound really freaky. But let's face it: most parents were freaking out before we made it sound so formal.

So, we must remind them Jesus is the only person who has ever kept all of his covenant commitments. We can step into regular acts of sacrificial love knowing we do so because he first loved us. The patterns and practices we live before our children are powerful. They have the power to shape our own affection and the affections of our children — not because the practices are magical — but because we are remembering and celebrating God's amazing salvation before the next generation. A child dedication service shouldn't be a guilt trip for our parents. Rather, it should call them into regular, sacrificial patterns of praying for, guiding, and teaching the gospel to their children.

"We Need the Church"

Grace doesn't come to those who deserve it. Grace comes to those who cry out. As Michael Horton writes:

> In a covenantal paradigm, I am bound intrinsically to God and to others in ways that transcend any good or service I can calculate. A total stranger rushes to a pond to pull out a young skater from the icy waters without running a cost-benefit analysis. The rescuer is not fulfilling a contractual obligation, but the command of God in his or her conscience that obligates a stranger to consider the endangered child a neighbor.[6]

Covenant obligations assume the truth that people need one another. Without neighbors who sacrificially love and rescue us, we're drowning. Specifically, we need help to confess we *are not* able to raise our children alone. Church leaders must signal to parents from the moment of their kids'

---

[6] Michael Horton, *Ordinary: Sustainable Faith in a Radical, Restless World* (Grand Rapids: Zondervan, 2014), 130.

conception that we know they need help. Our homes must be open, interdependent households not closed, nuclear units.

Church leaders must signal to parents from the moment of their kids' conception that we know they need help.

Megan and I are both type A. We religiously sit down every week to plan our finances and family calendar. We plan our vacations years in advance. But when our middle daughter, Lucy, was diagnosed with Autism Spectrum Disorder, we were stopped in our tracks. Our life was suddenly more than we could plan and manage.

SIDEBAR D: SAMPLE <u>CHURCH</u> VOWS FOR CHILD DEDICATION

Church, will you commit, in partnership with these parents, to instruct these children by word and example, in the truth of God's Word?

Will you commit to pray for these children — that they will grow to love Jesus and trust in him?

Will you commit to pray for these parents and encourage them as they face the trials of parenting?

If so, please read the following: "<u>With joy and thanksgiving, as Christ's church, with God's help, we promise to love, encourage, and support you as you follow Christ and train your children in the faith.</u>"

For years, Megan has taken Lucy to therapy appointments, cooked meals according to a strict diet, loved her stressed-out pastor husband, ministered to our church community herself, and worked through her own grief over Lucy's disabilities — all while being mother to two other typically developing (but still sinful) young girls. By four o'clock in the afternoon nearly every day, we're both exhausted.

One of the great graces in our life is that for six years, a group of young Christian women from Sojourn or Boyce College came to our home to help care for Lucy in the afternoons. These amazing ladies conducted a behavioral therapy program, potty-trained, and even taught Lucy a simple catechism. Most of the time we were able to use Medicaid funds to pay them. But one of the women, Kelly Stivers, kept working for us in a season when we lost our funding. She had our back even when there was seemingly nothing in it for her.

Whether it's times of adversity or prosperity, raising kids is a community project. Parents need the church. We need encouragement, accountability, and eyes to see what we can't see. That's why the child dedication plans you'll find in this booklet do not only call for a covenant commitment from parents, but they also call for a commitment from the entire church community. Every church member is responsible for the children dedicated at these services.

So, these are the goals for our child dedication services. *First*, God wants our kids, and ultimately their hearts and lives to belong to him. So, we confess together, "God, all we have — even our children — belongs to you. All we have is yours." *Secondly*, we don't just dedicate our children. We dedicate ourselves. We do this because we recognize our God-given responsibility as parents to love our kids with a commitment and loyalty. *Third,* we come to ask for help in the form of a commitment from our church, the believing community.

PHILOSOPHY (PART 2)

FOUR FREQUENTLY ASKED QUESTIONS ABOUT CHILD DEDICATION

1. Why Do You Perform Child Dedications Rather than Infant Baptisms? Isn't this just a "Dry Baptism"?

One key distinctive for Sojourn Network is believer's baptism. We are credo-baptists. We believe that baptism is a sign of the new covenant community, reserved for those who have believed upon Christ and experienced regeneration. The New Testament links this new covenant sign of baptism to the proclamation and trust in the gospel (Acts 2:38; 8:36).

But, at this point, you might be confused. I've been arguing above that the relationship between parents and their children is a *covenantal* one — as opposed to a consumer relationship. All family relationships are covenantal by their nature. But a child who is born physically into a believing family does not become a part of Jesus's new covenant family until he or she is born again (John 3:5–8). Paul tells us that Abraham is our model; the sign and seal of the covenant is given to those who have already been regenerated and justified (Romans 4:11).

Even we get confused. Once the week before a child dedication service, a Sojourn church elder, who will remain unnamed, invited the congregation back the following week for our infant baptism services. He never even caught or corrected his mistake!

Child dedication as we practice *is*, in fact, similar to the ceremony conducted by infant baptizers. That's why I quoted so many advocates of that position when explaining the covenantal nature of parenting above. But, biblically speaking, what infant baptizers practice is not truly baptism. I like to tell my Presbyterian friends that it's a "wet child dedication." Their practice confuses the grace of being born physically into a family who believes with the *greater* grace of being born spiritually into the family of faith.

For the sake of our kids' eternal souls, let's not mix this up. The confusion can be disastrous if it tempts parents to hold back from proclaiming the good news in their homes. As Stephen J. Wellum writes:

> To get baptism wrong is not a minor issue . . . It may even lead, if we are not careful, to a downplaying of the need to call our children to repentance and faith. Often Baptists are charged with not appreciating the place of their children in the covenant community. Not only does this charge miss the mark in fundamentally misunderstanding the nature of the new covenant community, but it also runs the danger of what is truly imperative — to call all people, including our children, to faith in our Lord Jesus Christ. It is only then that the

promise of the new covenant age becomes ours, for the promise is not only for us, but for our children and "for all who are far off, as many as the Lord our God will call" (Acts 2:39).[1]

2. Is this Even Biblical? I Don't See Any Verses in the Bible that Teach Child Dedication.

As I said, I don't have any Bible verses to reference here. I can't point to a passage which says, "Thou shalt have child dedication services." But I *do* know parents are tempted to think about their relationship with their kids as if it was a contract. And I also know nothing challenges consumer thinking quite like making really difficult covenant promises. It's true for marriage, and it's true for parenting too.

The child dedication covenant confirms this reality: parenting is a higher, self-sacrificial commitment. The sacred public vow helps us teach parents to practice regular patterns of sacrificial love from the very beginning of their parenting journey.

3. We're Dedicated to Our Kids Every Day. Why Do We Need a Service to Be Dedicated?

This question sounds like the one coming from the young guy who says to his fiancée, "Why have a marriage ceremony? We

---

[1] Stephen J. Wellum, "Baptism and the Relationship Between the Covenants," in *Believer's Baptism: the Sign of the Covenant in Christ*, ed. Thomas R. Schreiner and Shawn D. Wright (B&H, 2006), 169–170.

love each other. That's the important thing, right?" Making a public declaration *does* heighten the commitment. This is similar to the truth: when you write things down, you're more likely to actually do them. It is appropriate to experience a level of fear and reverence about heightened accountability and obligation. But in our culture, people are sometimes afraid that formalizing a relationship will destroy its intimacy, spontaneity, and fun, as well.

Yet the opposite is the case: The grace-based nature of the covenant commitment frees us from having to prove ourselves, and this ultimately leads to greater intimacy. It's true with marriage.

> When dating or living together, you have to prove your value daily by impressing or enticing. You have to show that the chemistry is there and the relationship is fun and fulfilling, or it will end quickly. We are still basically in a consumer relationship, and that means constant promotion and marketing. The legal bond of marriage, however, creates a space of security where we can open up and reveal our true selves. We can be vulnerable, no longer having to keep up facades.[2]

We don't have to keep selling ourselves. This is why lovers have an instinctive tendency to make promises to one another — "I will always love you" — at the height of passion (Song of Songs 8:6–7). They know, if only intuitively, that commitment and intimacy go together.

---

[2] Keller, *The Meaning of Marriage*, 89.

In a similar way, I believe that seeing parenting as a covenant, which is the goal of making a public commitment, will free us from the pressure to get everything right with our parenting. We can receive the authority, influence, and responsibility we have as a gift, but we can also receive how our kids turn out as a gift. In a fallen world, some kids will be sick and some kids will fall away from the faith. We can never accomplish all of our good goals. But a covenant way of thinking frees us to be thankful and enjoy God's good gifts when they come. If and when good things come, they are gifts from God. As Paul says in 1 Corinthians 4:7, "What do you have that you did not receive?"

4. Isn't this just a Sentimental Exercise?

At our church, the child dedication services have consistently been two of our top five high attendance services of the year — usually right behind Easter Sunday. We see child dedication as an incredible opportunity to proclaim the gospel to extended family members and equip parents to lead their children with loyalty and love. Before the child dedication service, we give invitations to the parents with children being dedicated to send out friends and family inviting them to the service. As you'll read about below, we also put together a child dedication class/small group. The goal is to make that time into, well, into a party — celebrating the new life God has given to the families in our church. We want it to be a time of gospel encouragement and celebration for our parents. We've found that this has been one of the most fruitful things we've done as a family ministry.

PROCESS (PART 1)

EVENT PLANNING TIMELINE AND CHECKLIST

In the checklist on the following pages, you'll see some of the details that go into our child dedication planning.

Annually

- **Schedule** one or two Sundays during the church year to celebrate child dedication with your church community. Coordinate with your church's preaching schedule and the community calendar. We're often thinking about two Sundays in a row so that the dedication class or small group study can be placed on the previous week. If necessary, be sure to reserve a classroom for the dedication class in addition to the time on the calendar.
- **Celebrate.** When God gives new life to a church community, it's something to celebrate. As an advocate for this ministry, be sure to celebrate with

other key staff and pastors. Because we've made it a celebration, child dedication has become a model commissioning service for our community. We've modeled our installation of pastors and commissioning of missionaries and group leaders after what we do in these services.

12 Weeks Before

- **Build a team.** We recruit experienced parents from our church community to lead the class or small group study. We recruit a team to handle decorations and refreshments for the class as well. And we recruit a logistics/hospitality team for the child dedication service.
- **Set up a registration form**. Begin requesting pertinent information from the parents. You can find a sample form that we use to request this information in Appendix 1.

6–8 Weeks Before

- **Begin publicity**. Use whatever communication platforms you have available at your local church, including website communication, social media, posters, stage announcements, and the bulletin. Also, personally contact any parents who missed the last child dedication deadline.
- **Give a testimony or show a video.** Cast vision for the next child dedication by sharing its impact

through a word of testimony or a video. I've
included a sample parent testimony in Appendix 2.

- **Order door prizes**. If you plan to give away door
prizes at your child dedication class/small group,
this is the time to order them. We give away two
different parenting books, children's music CDs,
and diaper bag tags with our children's ministry
logo.

2 Weeks Before

- **Prepare the details for the class/small group.**
Print the class notes and begin preparing food and
decorations. Our hospitality team decorates the
room for the class like a baby shower with baby
toys, confetti, and balloons. The food includes
punch, coffee, muffins, cookies, fruit, mints, and
nuts.

- **Order gift Bibles.** We give a gift Bible to each
family at the dedication service. Your registrations
are starting to come in at this point. So, estimate
how many families will be participating in the
service and order the gift Bibles. We give away a
copy of *The Beginner's Gospel Story Bible* by Jared
Kennedy (New Growth, 2017), or *The Jesus
Storybook Bible* by Sally Lloyd-Jones (Zondervan,
2007) to every family who participates in the
dedication service.

- **Print and mail invitations.** *If invitations are being
sent to extended family and friends, they should be printed
and mailed now.* In Appendix 3, I've included two

sample invitations that we've used in the past. When we've lacked administrators to fill out, print, and mail the invitations, we print blank invitations and give them to parents at the child dedication class along with stamped envelopes.

Sunday Before (Child Dedication Class)

- **Close registration.** This is the published deadline for submitting the registration form and information for the gift booklet. We regularly give parents some grace until the end of the following day, but this is the published deadline.
- **Conduct the dedication class.** Be sure the notes are printed. Be sure that the teaching, door prizes, refreshments, and decorations are ready. Be sure to inform the parents where to meet pastors / hospitality team prior to the service on the following week.

1–Week Prior

- **Choose a liturgy.** Decide on the service liturgy for the following Sunday. You will find sample liturgies in Appendix 4. Review this liturgy with the pastors and worship leadership for any updating.
- **Print the gift booklets**. If you giving away a gift booklet to parents, this is the time to print them to have them ready for the service.

- **Send parents a reminder** with details about where to meet with pastors prior to the service. Include the presentation script in your e-mail so the parents can review it and ensure their child's name is spelled correctly and gender is correctly identified. You can find a sample parent reminder e-mail in Appendix 5.

- **Wrap the gift Bibles.** It is an added encouragement to fill out the dedication section at the front of the gift Bible with a note of encouragement from your lead pastor, family pastor, or a children's ministry staff member.

- **Prepare the presentation slides.** We include the call and response for the parents and congregation on the slides. See the liturgies in Appendix 4. We also include a picture and the complete name for each child being dedicated.

- **Rehearse the dedication liturgy with any staff members involved.** Just as with a wedding, it can help the ceremony go more smoothly to do a walk-through a few days before. Practice saying the children's names, and practice where all leadership will stand on the stage.

On Dedication Sunday

- **Meet with the parents before the service.** Meet to pray with parents before the service. Also, take this time to walk the parents through the entire service. Over-explain. Clarify again where you will be asking them to stand. Note: If more than five families are participating, it is helpful to put masking tape down on the stage or floor to show each family where they are to stand when their names are read. Be sure to clarify the pronunciation of names and encourage the parents that they can take their kids to the nursery immediately following the dedication.

- **Reserve seats.** Reserve a section for the dedicating parents to sit and for their invited guests. We use the wrapped gift Bibles/gift booklets to reserve the section for the parents and extra gift booklets and signage to reserve the section for extended families and guests. We ask key leaders such as pastors' wives and deacons to stand in these areas to welcome the family members. This is an important opportunity to build relationships with family members who may not know Christ or who may be visiting your church for the first time.

Four Mistakes of Child Dedication

- **Don't be legalistic about the membership requirement.** Child dedication is not a sacrament. I repeat: child dedication is not a sacrament. We announce publicly that this is limited to members because that's who our membership has the clearest biblical obligation to support. But we're careful not to shame a member in process or regular attender who wants to commit to raise their child with love and loyalty. In fact, we're thrilled

about it. If they register, we welcome them to
participate.

- **Don't make dress or attire too formal.** Child
  dedication should be for everyone — from every
  economic situation. Don't let a formal dress code
  be a barrier that keeps a poor family from
  participating (James 2:1–4).

- **Don't lie about a child's cuteness.** Some kids are
  cute. Some aren't. Parents know. Guard your
  integrity.

- **Don't forget to coach parents on what is
  appropriate to share.** If you're going to put baby
  pictures on presentation slides, coach parents
  about what's appropriate. You don't need pictures
  of naked babies. Similarly, churches sometimes
  give parents an opportunity to share the story of
  how they chose their child's name — some share
  the stories publicly in the service; we share them
  with the dedicating families as part of a gift booklet.
  Be clear that when you ask for a naming story, you
  aren't asking for the conception story.

Four Keys of Child Dedication

- **Double-check pronunciation.** Knowing and
  remembering names is one of the best ways to help
  someone feel welcomed and loved. Listen. Repeat
  it back. Take notes in your copy of the liturgy.
  Practice it. Then, double-check on the day of the
  service.

- **Remember those who experience brokenness.** Any time you celebrate a biblical ideal, there will be a tendency for those whose life circumstances don't correspond with the ideal to feel judged — even when the brokenness they experience is no fault of their own. At child dedication, take just a moment to remember single parents, broken homes. Mention these families in your public prayers, and be patient with a parent who isn't immediately comfortable with participating. One single mom at our church waited until her child was nearly five to dedicate because it felt so embarrassing to stand in the front by herself without a husband. We didn't rush her. When she finally decided to go forward, her ex-husband came to the service. It was the first time he'd been to church and heard the gospel in years. Afterward, our team was able to celebrate God's providence in her delay and his presence to hear the gospel.

- **Practice hospitality.** This is a time to roll out the red carpet for extended family and friends. The way we welcome is a demonstration of our love and desire for these families to experience Christ.

- **Share with vulnerability and point to Jesus.** When you teach the dedication class or lead the congregation, be vulnerable. Honesty about your personal parenting struggles and need for grace will encourage the parents who are dedicating to offer themselves to God and trust Jesus for their parenting journey.

PROCESS (PART 2)

CHILD DEDICATION CLASS /
SMALL GROUP STUDY

Fully committing to child dedication services means that you're going to need to teach your people what it means to have a child (and a family) dedicated to the Lord *and* what it means to be embedded in the life of a local church.

Here are four group studies we've written to help you do this.

Our Kids Belong to God (Session 1)

Unless the LORD builds the house,
the builders labor in vain. (Psalm 127:1)

📖 **Read Psalm 127**

Our kids don't belong to us. They belong to God. Yet God has entrusted these kids to us. Psalm 127 explains, "Children are a heritage from the Lord. They are a reward from him." It is true. Kids are God's gift to us. But, as with every gift he gives, we are stewards. The older our kids get, the more it becomes clear that we can't control their destiny. Our kids' future, health, skill, will, and desires for life, who they will choose as a spouse, and even how long they will live — all of this belongs to God.

Do you struggle to believe this truth? Has it impacted the kinds of dreams that you have and goals you set for your children? When we fail to remember that our kids belong to God, we are tempted to think our success as parents will be measured by our kids' success. But apart from his grace our labors are in vain. God wants us to be faithful, but he wants us to let him be in control of our kids' lives. Consider the list of "good goals gone bad" below. Which of these goals has distracted you the most from the truth that your kids belong to God?

> **God wants us to be faithful, but he wants us to let him be in control of our kids' lives.**

(?) *Group Discussion*

Which one of these goals is most tempting for you? Why?[1]

Kids with Skills: I must enlist my child in as many activities (athletic, artistic, musical, etc.) as time may or may not allow. I measure my success by the number of activities

---

[1] This list of "good goals gone bad" is adapted from Tedd Tripp, *Shepherding a Child's Heart* (Shepherd Press, 2001), 40ff.

in which my son is involved. I measure his success by his mastery of skills and abilities.

Psychologically Adjusted Kids: Nothing is more important than building my child's self-esteem and training her to be effective with people. If she is confident, outgoing, and NOT spoiled, then I've been successful as a parent.

Christian Kids: My parenting rises or falls on getting my kids saved as soon as possible and by any means possible. I've been faithful as a parent so long as we're doing family worship nightly and my fifth grader is fluent in the catechism. What makes me a successful parent is seeing my kids in heaven one day.

Well-Behaved Kids: I feel good about myself when my child has poise, is kind, and she converses with respect to others. I'm winning when she's hospitable and serves her friends. I prepare my children to respond well to every conceivable situation or circumstance. I'm successful when my son responds obediently to my instruction with a great attitude.

Healthy Kids: I'll stop at nothing so that my kids are healthy, well-functioning, and safe from suffering. I measure my success by my ability to prepare well-balanced meals for our family in accordance with the most healthful diet. I know I'm succeeding because my child meets developmental goals and avoids illness.

Smart Kids: There are no lengths to which I won't go to prepare my kids for educational success. Their SAT/ACT score is my justification, and a college scholarship is my reward. I dream about them achieving academic awards, scholarly recognition, and eventually being recruited for privileged job opportunities.

 ### *Parent Mentorship*

If you are a newer parent, find a more seasoned parent in the church community — maybe someone in your community group or someone you serve with regularly on Sunday. You may want to meet one-on-one with a more seasoned parent, or you and your spouse may want to plan a double date with a couple who is a few steps ahead of you in raising their family. Take them out to coffee or dinner and ask them to share with you the parenting experiences that have most impacted them spiritually.

If you are a more seasoned parent, seek out a new parent and ask them what keeps them up at night about starting a family. Sympathize with them, and take time to encourage them and point them to trust in Jesus. Then, pray for their marriage and their kids.

I Will Commit to Love through Prayer (Session 2)

by Megan Kennedy

> *He is like a tree*
> *planted by streams of water*
> *that yields its fruit in its season,*
> *and its leaf does not wither.*
> *In all that he does, he prospers. (Psalm 1:3)*

📖 *Read Psalm 1*

One of the most basic and important ways that we love our children is through prayer. We can't love our children well if we don't think of them and make requests for them in the context of our vertical relationship with our heavenly Father. But if we're honest, prayer is one of the hardest things to do consistently and intentionally. Why is this the case? In this section, I want to do two things. First, I will overview some lies we believe that keep us from prayer. Second, since God's Word and prayer is the primary way to love your children in the context of your relationship with God, I want to show you how to use the Psalms as a tool for praying for your kids.

> **One of the most basic and important ways that we love our children is through prayer.**

❓ *Group Discussion*

> *I've listed seven lies that keep us from prayer below.*
> *Which one is most tempting for you?*
> *Take time to confess this to God.*[2]

---

[2] The quotes are from Paul E. Miller, *A Praying Life: Connecting with God in a Distracting World* (NavPress, 2009). For further study on prayer, see *Psalms: The Prayerbook of the Bible* by Dietrich Bonhoeffer (Augsberg / Fortress, 1974); *A Father's Guide to Blessing His Children* by David Michael (Children Desiring God, 1999), and *Bible Doctrine: Essential Teachings of the Christian Faith* by Wayne Grudem and Jeff Purswell (Zondervan, 1999), pp. 158–167.

1. "God is indifferent to my prayers." Why should I pray since God already knows what he's going to do? What difference does it make?"

This lie is a temptation to be cynical. Some say, "Prayer doesn't change anything. It just changes you." But if we give our kids good gifts, how much more will our heavenly Father give to us when we ask? We must pray to God with expectation even though we don't fully understand how it all works. *Pray Psalm 34.*

2. "God is impersonal and distant." He isn't close to me. What's the difference between praying and just hoping for things? Does God really care?"

Sometimes we struggle to believe that God is good, personal, and intimate. So, we won't come to Him. The good news is that God has come to us in Jesus. We can pray with confidence that God is near because he showed us his love at the cross. *Pray Psalm 139.*

3. "God's world and the real world aren't connected." Can I talk to God about everything? Shouldn't I just pray about spiritual things? Does everyday stuff matter to God?"

The Bible speaks against the distinction between *sacred* and *secular.* So, we can pray about anything, because God is involved in every aspect of our lives. *Pray Psalm 104.*

4. "I don't know what to pray for. What if I pray something that isn't God's will?" Why are we afraid to be honest with God about what we really want? Because we are terrified to admit our desires are often selfish, petty, and lame. If we could control God and make him answer the way we want, praying would be easy. But when we stop protecting ourselves and just ask him, we put the answer in his hands. We can pray honestly for our desires — our kids' good health, their academic success, and their salvation — because God knows what is best. *Pray Psalm 103.*

5. "I know I should pray, but it feels like an obligation." When I pray, I feel holy. When I don't, I feel guilty."

Deep down, we believe prayer makes us better Christians. It is something we do for God; something that makes us more spiritual. But sometimes we focus too much on the prayer itself instead of God. Our goal is to experience him as we are. Dare to pray imperfectly as a sinner who can approach God in Jesus' name. *Pray Psalm 51.*

6. "I don't need to pray, because I can handle it." Or, if we do pray, we're essentially saying, "Lord, please bless my efforts." We think of ourselves as God. We have our lives under control. Paul Miller writes, "If you are not praying, then you are quietly confident that time, money, and talent are all you need in life." But, in reality, we are desperate for God. If dependence on God is our goal, then weakness is our advantage. Let go of your anxieties in prayer, because God is the one in control, not us. *Pray Psalm 131.*

7. "I don't have time to pray, because I have so much to do." If we love people, we are going to be busy. Paul Miller says, "Prayer doesn't offer us a less busy life. It offers us a less busy heart." By praying, we can experience God and his eternal peace in the midst of our busy lives. Prayer gives us a heavenly perspective and helps us live for eternal rewards. Pray as one who is not of this world. *Pray Psalm 23.*

Pray the Psalms

The Psalms provide a model for our prayers, and we can pray them as blessings over our children as well. Here is a model blessing based on Psalm 1. Write out one of the Psalms above on a notecard and pray it over your child this week.

May the Lord bless you! May the Lord give you courage not to walk with the wicked, faith not to stand with sinners, and resolve not to sit with mockers. May you always delight in Gods' law and meditate on it daily. May you be like a fruitful tree planted by streams of water!

I Will Commit to Love through Planning (Session 3)

And these words that I command you today shall be on your heart. You shall teach them diligently to your children, and shall talk of them when you sit in your house, and when you walk by the way, and when you lie down, and when you rise. (Deuteronomy 6:6–7)

Read Deuteronomy 6:1–9

When you come forward with your child at our dedication service, you will see the following on the screen:

Parents, will you entrust your children to God — to His providential plan and care?
Will you commit to pray for them and teach them to pray?
Will you commit to instruct your children by word and example, in the truth God's Word?
Then, you will be prompted to say, "With God's help, we will."

The commitment has three parts. First, we commit that our children belong to God and not to us. Secondly, we commit to love them through prayer. Prayer, as discussed in the previous section, is the primary way to show our children love in the context of our vertical relationship with the heavenly Father. Finally, we also commit to loving our children by instructing them through our words and example.

Do these commitments sound scary? Maybe they should. You are making a huge commitment — entrusting, praying, disciplining, instructing in word and example. Committing to all of that sounds really freaky. But most of you were freaking out before we made it sound so formal. If you are completing this study, you probably don't need to be told to be a good and godly parent. But knowing you should teach your kids about God isn't the same thing as knowing how. So, in this section, I want to show you a tool on how to map out an intentional parenting plan.

> **Knowing you should teach your kids about God isn't the same thing as knowing how.**

(?) *Group Discussion*

Pick a day for yourself and your family five years from now. Use this list of questions to help you envision that day. Then, share it with your group.[3]

Questions about Your Immediate Family:

---

[3] These questions for envisioning are from "Reverse Engineering Your Life" (Mars Hill Church, 2007).

- Do you have time alone by yourself?
- If married, do you have a regular date night?
- How often do you pray together with your spouse?
- How can you take better care of your spouse?
- What has helped your love to grow over the past five years? How has your home become a place for unplanned connecting? What brings you together?
- How many children will you have in five years?
- How old will your kids be on the date you're envisioning?
- How will they be educated at that time?
- What special attention will each child need regarding their maturation up to that day?
- Which family and friends are you closest with as a family?

Questions about Your Extended Family:

- Which close relatives may not be living at this five-year planning mark?
- What is your relationship like with each family member (e.g., mom, dad, brother, sister, grandparent)?
- How has your family been included in your vacations and holidays?
- What has changed with your extended family over the past five years?

Questions about Your Personal Growth:

- What marriage or parenting books have you read?

- How many minutes do you read each day? When do you read? Where?
- What other learning experiences have shaped you (e.g., conferences, mentors, spiritual disciplines)?
- How is your physical and spiritual health at this five-year mark? What have you done to improve it?

 ## *Make a Plan*

Think through this same list of questions with your spouse, and pick three things that you would like to put into practice immediately to help move your family toward this vision. List them out here:

1. _____

_____

_____

2. _____

_____

_____

3. _____

_____

_____

Here are examples of what you might write:

1. Read a Bible storybook three times each week with my child.
2. Read a parenting book with my spouse this year.
3. Set aside one date night each quarter to talk with my spouse about our children's' future.

Next, write these three things on an index card. Put it somewhere where you will see and read it regularly (like your car dashboard). Ask a friend to hold you accountable.

Finally, pick a date six months from now to work through the questions again. Put that date in you and your spouse's calendar. How is your plan going? Are there things that need to be adjusted? Is it challenging? Is it too challenging? Make adjustments. Do you need to scrap your plan and start over (e.g., my kids are at a new stage, my family dynamics have changed)? If so, start reworking.

I Need the Church (Session 4)

> *He established a testimony in Jacob*
> *and appointed a law in Israel. (Psalm 78:5a)*

 Read Psalm 78:1–8

Parents share their responsibility with the entire church community. Training children is a community project because we need each other. We need one another's encouragement, one another's accountability, and one another's eyes to see what we can't see.

Every church member is responsible for the children who will be dedicated at the upcoming service. So, after the children are presented, every Christian present will be invited to stand. Then, a pastor will say the following:

Parents, look around you. You are not alone. This is your community of faith.

Church, will you commit, in partnership with these parents, to instruct these children by word and example in the truth of God's Word?

Will you commit to pray for these children — that they will grow to love Jesus and trust in him?

Will you commit to pray for these parents and encourage them as they face the trials of parenting?

If so, please read the following:

With joy and thanksgiving,
As Christ's church,
With God's help,
We promise to love, encourage, and support you
As you follow Christ and train your children in the faith.

The family and the church were created to work together, but often we're tempted away from this balance. Sometimes parents are tempted to think that training kids in the Bible is the responsibility of "professionals" at the church. So, parents will faithfully bring their kids to church gatherings every weekend but never mention God throughout

The church needs families, and families need the church.

the week. On the other end of the spectrum, there are parents who struggle to trust the church community and pull their children out of all kids and youth activities to disciple their kids alone. Neither way is biblical. Neither is ideal. The church needs families, and families need the church. We need each other like two pedals on a bike.

The church is an important part of God's plan, and so is the family. Christ loved his bride, the church, and established her with several purposes. It is easy to understand the church's responsibility to teach adults, but notice in the psalm that both family and the community have been given the task to teach young people. Those of you around kids can see God's wisdom in this plan. Here are just a few reasons why church ministry to children and students is needed:[4]

> The church is needed to surround young people with godly adults who can provide love and care, truth they can build their lives on, and a model to follow (1 Corinthians 11:1; 1 Peter 5:2).

> The church is needed to reach out and model the gospel for children who do not have Christian parents (Matthew 19:14; 28:19–20).

> The church is needed to reinforce a biblical view of the world. A child will sometimes listen to a children's or youth ministry volunteer even though they have heard

---

[4] Adapted from Steve Wright and Chris Graves, *ApParent Privilege* (InQuest, 2008), 99–110.

that same truth from their parent again and again (2 Timothy 4:2).

When there is a major family conflict, the church is needed to be a neutral third party serving as an impartial advisor between parents and kids (2 Corinthians 5:18).

The church is needed to connect believing young people with other Christians who support, encourage, and keep them accountable (Hebrews 10:25).

The church is needed to provide opportunities for young people to use their gifts to serve (1 Corinthians 12).

The church is needed because she fights for truth and sound doctrine. The church protects families from being drawn away by false teaching (1 Timothy 3:15).

The church is needed because spiritual growth generally happens within the context of community (Ephesians 4:11–16).

But the church is not only for our kids. Parents need the church just as desperately. When the responsibility to teach our children about God is overwhelming, the church is there to help. The church teaches us how to teach and trains us in how to train. The church is both a gift to received and a blessing to be to others. The church is our partner in the task of teaching our children about God.

(?) *Group Discussion*

Do you tend to have a "drop-off" mentality — thinking of the church's ministers as professionals?

Or do you have a "nuclear family" mentality — thinking you can handle things on your own without the church?

How do the truths taught in this lesson inform and change your thinking?

Plan a Celebration!

Plan a baby shower, birthday party, or just throw a party to celebrate the life of a child / children in your community group. Pray and thank God for putting a gospel community in the lives of the kids. Then, take time to pray a community blessing over the children.

CONCLUSION

I began this book by asking you to imagine taking a trip to the grocery store with your kids. Recently, I used that same illustration in a workshop with a small group of parents. They looked at me with blank stares and later confessed: "The illustration made sense, but we've never taken our kids to the grocery store. Wal-Mart and Amazon deliver!"

That was a humbling reminder both of my increasing age of the fact that the world of parenting is always changing. What young parents in your church encounter as their kids grow up may differ radically from your experience or from the experience of parents who are only a few years older.

But some things won't change. We must encourage every generation of mothers and fathers with basic truth about what it means to steward their role as parents. We must teach them:

- Your kids are gifts from God and not the products of your success!
- You are responsible to sacrificially love your child, so make it a life-long commitment.

- And, finally, you can't do this alone! So, call upon your church community for help.

Our prayer is that this book inspires you to teach these truths by planning a Child Dedication service for your local church. Our goal has been to give you the practical help that's needed to do just that. If you're planning a service for the first time, follow the checklist, use the preparation study guide, and adapt the sample liturgies for your context. Through faithful acts of discipleship like this, God is at work to transform the next generation so . . . *they in turn would tell their children. Then they would put their hope in God and would not forget his works but keep his commandments (Psalm 78:6-7).*

PRACTICES

APPENDICES

APPENDIX ONE

SAMPLE REGISTRATION FORM

Sign-Up for the [Include Date] Child Dedication!

Thank you for your interest in the Child Dedication (for children of members or those currently involved in the membership process) scheduled for Sunday, [Month, Date, Year] at [Church Location].

As parents, you have an opportunity to express thanks to God for the gift of children, declare your commitment to the gospel as parents, and ask the church for help and accountability as you seek to parent with wisdom.

Thank you for taking time to complete all information below. Stars indicate required fields.

Parent's Name* (First, Last)

_____

Parent's Name (First, Last)

Child #1's Name* (First, Middle, Last)

Child #2's Name (First, Middle, Last)

Child #3's Name (First, Middle, Last)

E-mail*

Phone Number*

[For multi-site and multi-service churches] Let us know the church and service time at which you plan to attend with your children on Dedication Sunday* **[List options]**

Please indicate the time you will attend the "First Steps for Child Dedication" class/small group. * [Note: We require the child dedication class as a pre-requisite for participating in dedication services.]

We request the following information to prepare a gift booklet for the parents who participate in the dedication service and their families. The booklet contains a baby picture of each child along with a paragraph birth/adoption announcement according to the format described below. We also use this information to prepare a presentation slide used to announce the child in the service.

The following information is for the gift booklet you will receive at the dedication service. Registrations that are received AFTER **[Clear Deadline]** can participate in the dedication but will not be included in the gift booklet.

Please write a 100-word paragraph about your child. Write it as if you were going to read it. Please include the following information: *

_____

_____

_____

_____

_____

_____

Presentation introduction including your child's full name and gender in the following format (Jared and Megan Kennedy present their daughter, Elisabeth Mercy Kennedy).

Why did you choose this name?

_____

_____

_____

Your baby's birth date

_____

Parents' and siblings' names

_____

_____

_____

What lessons have you/your family learned since having this child?

_____

_____

_____

_____

A Bible verse that has particular meaning for you and your family.

_____

_____

_____

_____

_____

Please provide us with a digital picture of just your child for the gift booklet (due before **[Clear Deadline]** and the dedication service presentation slide. If possible, please convert the picture to a JPEG (.JPG) format and name it according to the following format (LAST NAME_FIRST NAME_MIDDLE NAME.JPG). *

We request the following information to prepare invitations that are sent to the friends and close families of those who participate in the dedication.

List up to 10 names and mailing addresses of family/friends you would like for us to invite to the service for you. We will mail invitations for all registrations received BEFORE **[Clear Deadline]**.

_____

_____

_____

_____

_____

_____

_____

_____

_____

_____

_____

_____

Do you have a godparent or grandparent who would like to stand with you and pray for your child during the service?**

_____

_____

_____

_____

**This is not something we've done at Sojourn Community Church in Louisville, but many churches have found including a member of the extended church family to be meaningful.

APPENDIX TWO

ONE PARENT'S TESTIMONY

Like most parents, I suppose, the birth of our first child was simultaneously the most exciting and most terrifying thing that had ever happened to my wife and I. We spent nine months planning, praying, and preparing for him to arrive. We read books and talked to other parents to find out "what to expect" but we could never really get a clear answer. We have always desired to raise our children in a home centered on Christ, but we weren't really sure what that looked like.

We knew a baby dedication service was a good place to start, but like most things with kids, we didn't know what to expect. I remember talking with my wife about the class we were required to take before the service. We pondered what the content would be. We guessed maybe a list of requirements for parents at Sojourn. Perhaps they'd teach us how to have family devotions. Maybe they'll give us a theology lesson on why we don't do infant baptism.

While we certainly should have seen it coming, one thing we didn't consider was that the class might be designed for was encouraging us in the gospel. We sat for an hour and a half and listened to how the gospel sets us free as parents, how the Lord is in control of our child and how we didn't need to have family devotions figured out. We were given tools to parent with but reminded that they were just tools and not a rulebook.

The dedication service continued the theme of encouragement. I can't tell you how assuring it is for a scared dad to stand before his church and hear them promise to have my back. Taylor and I were so grateful for the prayers offered over us and the love shown during that time.

We left the dedication service still having no clue what we were doing as parents. But we also left with the confidence that the gospel had set us free from the burden of knowing it all and that our church family had our back every step of the way.

Stuart Owens
Dad at Sojourn Community Church, Midtown in Louisville, KY

APPENDIX THREE

SAMPLE INVITATIONS

Blank invitation with a floral design:

We will thank God for
giving us our new child.

We will commit to love
this child like Jesus does.

We will ask our Christian
community to help us as
we raise our child with
love and joy.

You are invited to the dedication of:

_____

_____

Date

_____

Service Time

Sojourn Community Church
Midtown Campus
930 Mary Street
Louisville, KY 40204

Pre-printed invitation with a script design:

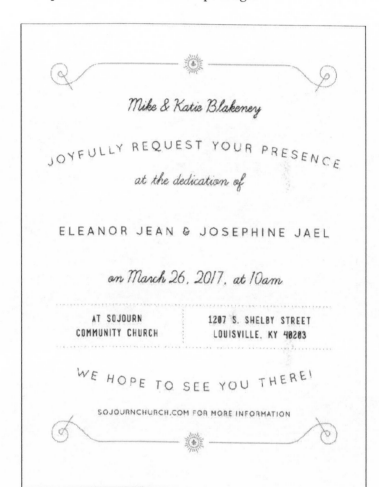

Mike & Katie Blakeney

JOYFULLY REQUEST YOUR PRESENCE

at the dedication of

ELEANOR JEAN & JOSEPHINE JAEL

on March 26, 2017, at 10am

AT SOJOURN COMMUNITY CHURCH	1207 S. SHELBY STREET LOUISVILLE, KY 40203

WE HOPE TO SEE YOU THERE!

SOJOURNCHURCH.COM FOR MORE INFORMATION

APPENDIX FOUR

SAMPLE LITURGY FOR THE CHILD DEDICATION SERVICE

The child dedication liturgy includes an introduction section (I've provided three options below), the presentation of the families, the parent commitment, and the church community commitment. Child Dedication Sunday is a fun day. Own these words with strength and joy.

Option 1

[Bolded text is projected]

We celebrate new life on Child Dedication Sunday. We love children! In Genesis, God gave the command to "be fruitful and multiply" and we take God's commands seriously.

Here is the word of the Lord:

Give ear, O my people, to my teaching;
incline your ears to the words of my mouth!
I will open my mouth in a parable;

I will utter dark sayings from of old,
things that we have heard and known,
   that our fathers have told us.
We will not hide them from their children,
   but tell to the coming generation
the glorious deeds of the LORD, and his might,
   and the wonders that he has done.

He established a testimony in Jacob
   and appointed a law in Israel,
which he commanded our fathers
   to teach to their children,
that the next generation might know them,
   the children yet unborn,
and arise and tell them to their children,
   so that they should set their hope in God
and not forget the works of God,
   but keep his commandments;
and that they should not be like their fathers,
   a stubborn and rebellious generation,
a generation whose heart was not steadfast,
   whose spirit was not faithful to God.
   (Psalm 78:1–7)

In this passage we see three huge things:

- *First, we see God's desire for every generation.* God wants every generation to know and trust in him — not forgetting what he has done to rescue and save, but remembering him and keeping his commandments. This is God's goal for every generation.

- *Secondly, we see how God gets this done* — through parents committing to continually pass on to their children the gospel truth that has been entrusted to them. We teach our kids in the unplanned moments in our cars as we drive along the road, at our child's bedside, at the breakfast table, and when they are throwing a tantrum at the grocery store. We also teach them in those planned moments when you pull out a Bible storybook and read to your child before bed. Teaching our kids about God involves us parents intentionally speaking about the gospel and sharing our lives with our children. It is a great responsibility. Parenting is one of the greatest things in life we can do, and it is one of the hardest.

- *Finally, by God's grace, we see that this is a responsibility we share this with the entire church family.* God puts us together in the church because we need each other. In training our children, we need one another's encouragement, one another's accountability, and one another's eyes to see what we can't see.

Remember: God wants generation after generation to know and trust him. And he will accomplish this through us.

[Transition] Parents, you are saying today, "I want to pass on the truth of the gospel to the next generation. And I need God to do this through me."

Option 2

[Bolded text is projected]

At our church, we LOVE to celebrate. Don't you just love getting gifts! Child Dedication is a celebration of new life, a gift! The Bible says it like this:

Children are a gift from the LORD;
they are a reward from him. (Psalm 127:3, NLT)

We celebrate child dedication, because, as the Psalm says, children are gifts from God. The Bible teaches us that salvation is a gift from God as well.

We want to steward both of these gifts by walking alongside our kids and helping them un-wrap the gift of salvation in their lives. In child dedication, we are committing before God, one another, and the watching world that we will love our children as gifts from God himself. We will steward our children for God's glory, their good, and as a blessing to the world.

[Transition] Parents, you are saying today, "I want to pass on gospel truth to the next generation. I need God to do this through me.

Option 3

[Bolded text is projected]

Today is a day that we say, "Congratulations!" Thanks be to God for the arrival and adoption of these little bundles of hope. Soak up every ounce of joy and elation and starry-eyed wonder at the miracle of these children. We'll all be watching as the terror sets in.

Parenthood is going to be the hardest thing you've ever done, but it's also one of the greatest things. It's worth every bit of the blood, sweat, and tears that are to come.

By coming forward today, you are confessing that you believe in a stewardship vision of parenting. By coming forward . . .

- *First, you are announcing that your children don't belong to you.* Yes, you will make promises to God about how you will raise your kids, but you're also confessing that in those responsibilities you're a steward. Your kids belong to a promise-keeping Father who is even more faithful than you.

- *Second, you are committing to faithfulness even when suffering comes.* Your babies are beautiful. We're about to "Oooh" and "Aaah" over their photos. And I don't mean to rain on the parade of your joy, but I do feel compelled to share the bad news, too: Your kids might break your heart. Actually, they *will* break your heart. Somehow. Somewhere. Maybe more than once. To become a parent is to promise you'll love prodigal children. It will require absorbing all of your child's misplaced animosity and teenage angst; all his or her confused attempts to figure out who (and whose) he is. In those moments, Jesus' call to lay down your life and take up your cross will have a mundane particularity you could have never imagined. Remember your promise today to be faithful, and remember this final thing . . .

- *Today, you are claiming that you are NOT able to raise your child alone.* Child dedication is a sign that our homes are open, interdependent households, not closed, nuclear units. Child dedication is our church's way of signaling right from the get-go that *we know you need help!* We know you can't do this on your own. So we're not going to be surprised or disappointed or judgmental when you lean on us. We'll be there waiting.

[Transition] Parenthood is going to be the hardest thing you've ever done, but it's worth it. The Bible says . . .

Children are a gift from the LORD;
they are a reward from him. (Psalm 127:3, NLT)

One day, I believe (because it's already happening) that these little gifts will stand before this same congregation and in other churches like ours as beautiful, mystifying, wonderful young men and women. They'll confess (we pray), "Jesus is Lord." It's to that end that we make these commitments.

Presentation of the Families:

Parents, when I call your names, please come forward, stand here at the front and face out toward the gathering.

[Pictures and baby names on the screen. For each family, read something like the following]: *Justin and Alana Karl present their daughter, Eloise Parker Karl.*

Parents' Commitment:

Parents, please turn and face me. I have some weighty questions for you

> [On screen] **Parents, will you entrust your children to God — to his providential plan and care?**
> **Will you commit, with the help of this church community, to instruct your children by word and example, in the truth of God's Word?**
> **Will you commit to pray for them and teach them to pray?**

> [Not on screen] If so, say, "With God's help, we will."
> [Parents respond]

Community Commitment:

Parents, you just made a commitment to one of the greatest things we can do but one of the hardest things you can do. But the truth is, you are not alone.

People of God, I've got a pretty weighty question for you as well. In light of these parents stepping out in faith, we are going to step up as the church to support them."

Here is our question for you:

> [On screen] **Do you, the people of the Lord, promise to receive these children in love, pray for them, help instruct them in the faith, and encourage and sustain them in this fellowship of believers?**

If so, please read the following:

**With joy and thanksgiving, as Christ's church,
With God's help, we promise to love, encourage,
   and support you
As you follow Christ and train your children in the
   faith.**

Let us pray. [*Pray extemporaneously.*]

APPENDIX FIVE

SAMPLE PARENT REMINDER E-MAIL

Dear Parents,

I'm so excited about your participation in the Child Dedication Service this coming Sunday. These kids are a good gift from God to your family and our entire church community.

Please take some time to review the list of names at the bottom of this e-mail to ensure that you have been assigned to the correct service and your name(s) and your child's name are spelled correctly.

Then, as a reminder, don't forget these important notes for Sunday:

- **Please arrive 30 minutes before your service.** Meet at [designated location]. [Designated leader] will meet you there. She will be wearing a nametag and a blue Sojourn Kids T-shirt. [Adjust this to fit your context.]

- **Send your family and friends ahead to the service.** We will have an area reserved for them to sit.
- **We will walk together to the prayer chapel [or other designated meeting place].** [Designated person] will go over the order of service with you. I will pray with you, and then we will walk you to your assigned seats.
- **When your name is called, stand on the X marked with masking tape on the stage/floor.** Be sure to walk all the way across the stage/floor to the next unoccupied X. The service pastors will prompt you through the remainder of the ceremony.

Yours truly,
[Your name and title]

Here are the names for your review **[Include the full list of names for all services]**:

8:30 AM Service (2 families)
Jared and Rachel Davila present their son, Rhodes
    Cornell Davila
Justin and Alana Karl present their daughter, Eloise
    Parker Karl
10:00 AM Service (1 family)
Mike and Katie Blakeney present their daughters,
    Eleanor Jean and Josephine Jael Blakeney

APPENDIX SIX

PRAYER FOR OUR CHILDREN

Gracious God, Giver of all life,
We pray for these parents.
Give them wisdom and patience.
Let your peace and joy dwell in their homes.
Instruct them in your gospel truth.
Strengthen them in faith.
Sustain them through prayer.
Order their lives by love.
We pray for these children.
Be gracious to them.
Draw them to yourself.
Help them to love and trust Jesus.
We pray that you will grow them in faith,
So that they might be like arrows in your hand.
For Christ's sake, Amen.[1]

---

[1] You might consider printing this on the back cover of your bulletin.

ACKNOWLEDGMENTS

I am so grateful to be a part of a network that believes in mission fueled by gospel renewal. It has been a joy to serve our churches as a strategist. I am so thankful for Dave Harvey, Dave Owens, Mark Owens, Casey Smith, Whitney Bozarth, and Justin Karl for this project and for making it such a joy to serve our churches.

This book wouldn't have been possible without my wife, Megan, who wrote part of the study and helped me launch our first child dedication class at Sojourn in Louisville. I'm also grateful for everyone who has served as a Kids Director at each Sojourn congregation. Your faithful work planning Child Dedication Sundays has helped to make this a part of our culture that I'm honored to celebrate and share.

ABOUT THE AUTHOR

Jared Kennedy is the pastor of families at Sojourn Community Church — Midtown in Louisville, Kentucky, where he lives with his wife Megan and three daughters. He holds a Th. M. and M. Div. from The Southern Baptist Theological Seminary and has over a decade of experience leading family ministry. He is the author of *The Beginner's Gospel Story Bible* (New Growth Press, 2017).

Jared tweets at @JaredSKennedy and blogs at gospelcenteredfamily.com.

ABOUT SOJOURN NETWORK

Throughout the pages of the New Testament, and especially in the book of Acts, we observe a pattern: men and women, through prayer and dependence of God and empowered by the Spirit, are sent by God (often through suffering) to spread the Word of the Lord. As this great news of new life in Christ spread into the neighboring cities, regions, provinces, and countries, gatherings of new believers formed into local communities called churches. As these gatherings formed by the thousands in the first century, the early church — taking its cue from the scriptures — raised up qualified, called, and competent men to lead and shepherd these new congregations.

Two-thousand years later, God is still multiplying his gospel in and through his church, and the Good Shepherd is still using pastors to lead and shepherd God's people. In Sojourn Network, we desire to play our part in helping these pastors plant, grow, and multiply healthy churches.

We realize that only the Spirit can stir people's hearts and bring them into community with other believers in Jesus. Yet, by offering the pastors in our network a strong vision of planting, growing, and multiplying healthy churches and by providing them with thorough leadership assessment, funding for new churches and staff, coaching, training, renewal, and resources, we can best steward their gifts for the benefit and renewal of their local congregations.

Since 2011, our aim at Sojourn Network has been to provide the care and support necessary for our pastors to lead their churches with strength and joy — and to finish ministry well.

OTHER "HOW-TO" BOOKS

Here are the current books in the "How-To" series. Stay tuned for more.

Healthy Plurality = Durable Church: "How-To" Build and Maintain a Healthy Plurality of Elders by Dave Harvey

Life-Giving-Groups: "How-To" Grow Healthy, Multiplying Community Groups by Jeremy Linneman

Charting the Course: "How-To" Navigate the Legal Side of a Church Plant by Tim Beltz

Redemptive Participation: A "How-To" Guide for Pastors in Culture by Mike Cosper

Filling Blank Spaces: "How-To" Work with Visual Artists in Your Church by Michael Winters

Before the Lord, Before the Church: "How-To" Plan a Child Dedication Service by Jared Kennedy with Megan Kennedy

Sabbaticals: "How-To" Take a Break from Ministry before Ministry Breaks You by Rusty McKie

Leaders through Relationship: "How-To" Develop Leaders in the Local Church by Kevin Galloway

Raising the Dust: "How-To" Equip Deacons to Serve the Church by Gregg Allison & Ryan Welsh (forthcoming)

Healthy Plurality = Durable Church: "How-To" Build and Maintain a Healthy Plurality of Elders by Dave Harvey

Have you ever wondered what separates a healthy church from an unhealthy church when they have the same doctrine (and even methods) on paper? The long-term health and durability of a church simply cannot exceed the health of her elders who lead, teach, shepherd, and pray the church forward. Therefore, building and maintaining a healthy plurality of elders is the key to durability. Yet a healthy plurality is a delicate thing working through hardship and the difficulties of relationship while pursuing the noble task of eldership. If you wish to grow deeper in your theology of eldership to lead with a healthy, biblical vision of plurality, then this is your "How-To" guide.

Life-Giving-Groups: "How-To" Grow Healthy, Multiplying Community Groups by Jeremy Linneman

Cultivate life-giving, Christ-centered communities. After many years of leading small groups and coaching hundreds of small group leaders, pastor and writer Jeremy Linneman has come to a bold conviction: Community groups are the best place for us — as relational beings — to become mature followers of Christ. This short book seeks to answer two questions: How can our community groups cultivate mature disciples of Christ? And how can our groups grow and multiply to sustain a healthy church? Whether you are new to community groups or tired from years of challenging ministry, *Life-Giving Groups* is a fresh, practical invitation to life together in Christ.

Charting the Course: "How-To" Navigate the Legal Side of a Church Plant by Tim Beltz

Planting a church? It's time to plot the course toward legal validity.
Church planting is overwhelming enough before dealing with the legal and
business regulations of founding a church. *Charting the Course* is for anyone,
at any experience level to learn how to navigate the legal side of planting a
church.

Redemptive Participation: A "How-To" Guide for Pastors in Culture by Mike Cosper

Our culture is confused. And so are we. It's not just you or them. It's all of us. But we can move past confusion and into a place of careful discernment. *Redemptive Participation* brings awareness to the shaping forces in our current culture and how to connect these dynamics with our teaching and practice.

Filling Blank Spaces: "How-To" Work with Visual Artists in Your Church by Michael Winters

In the beginning, the earth was empty. Blank spaces were everywhere. *Filling Blank Spaces* addresses a topic that usually gets blank stares in the church world. But Winters is a seasoned veteran of arts ministry and has developed a premier arts and culture movement in the United States, without elaborate budgets or celebrity cameos. Instead, this guide gives a "How-To" approach to understanding visual art as for and from the local church, steering clear of both low-brow kitsch and obscure couture. If you are ready to start engaging a wider, and often under-reached, swath of your city, while awakening creative force within your local church, then this book is for you.

Before the Lord, Before the Church: "How-To" Plan a Child Dedication Service by Jared Kennedy with Megan Kennedy

Is child dedication just a sentimental moment to celebrate family with "oohs and ahhs" over the babies? Or is it a solemn moment before God and a covenanting one before the local church? Kennedy explains a philosophy of child dedication with poignant "How-To" plan for living out a powerful witness to Christ for one another and before the watching world. Whether you are rescuing various forms of child dedication from sentimentalism or perhaps sacrament, this book will guide you to faithful and fruitful ministry honoring God for the gift of children while blessing your church.

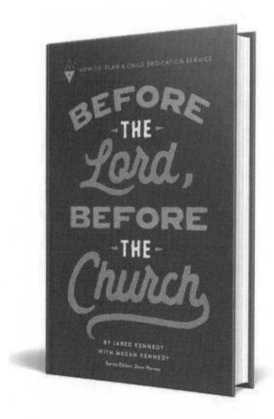

Sabbaticals: "How-To" Take a Break from Ministry before Ministry Breaks You by Rusty McKie

Are you tired and worn out from ministry? Isn't Jesus' burden supposed to be light? In the pressure-producing machine of our chaotic world, Jesus' words of rest don't often touch our life. As ministry leaders, we know a lot about biblical rest, yet we don't often experience it. The ancient practice of sabbath provides ample wisdom on how to enter into rest in Christ. *Sabbaticals* is a guide showing us how to implement Sabbath principles into a sabbatical as well as into the ebb and flow of our entire life.

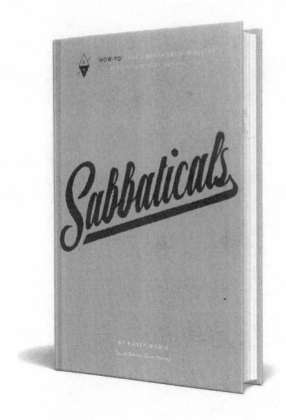

Leaders through Relationship: "How-To" Develop Leaders in the
Local Church by Kevin Galloway

The church needs more godly leaders. But where do they come from?
Some people read leadership books in a season of rest and health. But if
we're honest, most often we read leadership books when we're frazzled,
when we see the problems around us but not the solutions. If you're feeling
the leadership strain in your church, let Kevin Galloway show you a way
forward, the way of Jesus, the way of personally investing in leaders who
then invest in other leaders—because making an intentional plan to
encourage and train leaders, is not a luxury; it's mission critical, for your
health and the health of your church.

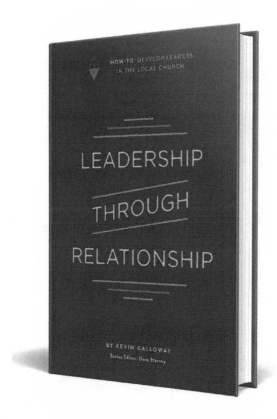

Raising the Dust: "How-To" Equip Deacons to Serve the Church by Gregg Allison & Ryan Welsh (forthcoming)

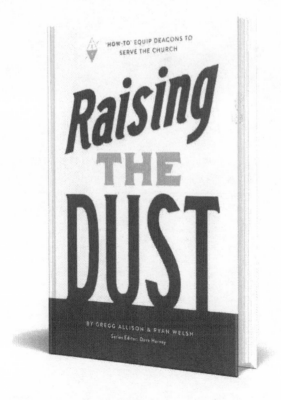